Let us Follow Him

Henryk Sienkiewicz

Translated by Jeremiah Curtin

Originally published in 1897

The period of "Let Us Follow Him" is that of the death of Christ. Antea, the wife of a Roman patrician, ill with terrible visions, is advised by a physician to seek the air of Jerusalem. There she and her husband meet Pilate, who tells them of the doctrine of the Nazarene, Jesus, and his condemnation to death. They are present at the Crucifixion, and Antea gives honor to the condemned Nazarene, saying, "Thou art Truth."

TABLE OF CONTENTS

CHAPTER I

Caius Septimius Cinna was a Roman Patrician. He had spent his youth in the legions and in severe camp-life. Later he returned to Rome to enjoy glory, luxury, and a great though somewhat shattered fortune. He used and abused at that time everything which the gigantic city could offer.

His nights were spent at feasts in lordly suburban villas; his days in sword practice with fencers, in discussions with rhetors at the baths, where disputes were held, and where the scandal of the city and the world was related, in circuses, at races, at the struggles of gladiators, or among Greek musicians, Thracian soothsayers, and wonderful dancing-girls from the islands of the Archipelago. He inherited from the renowned Lucullus, a relative on the mother's side, a love for exquisite dishes. At his table were served Grecian wines, Neapolitan oysters, Numidian mice, and locust fat preserved in honey from Pontus.

Whatever Rome possessed Cinna must have, beginning with fish of the Red Sea, and ending with white ptarmigans from the banks of the Borysthenes (Dnieper). He made use of things not only as a soldier run riot, but as a patrician who passes the measure. He had instilled into himself, or had perhaps even roused in himself, a love for the beautiful,—a love for statues rescued from the ruins of Corinth, for pitchers from Attica, for Etruscan vases from foggy Sericum, for Roman mosaics, for fabrics brought from the Euphrates, for Arabian perfumes, and for all the peculiar trifles which filled the void of patrician life.

He knew how to talk of these trifles, as a specialist and connoisseur, with toothless old men, who decked out their baldness in wreaths of roses when going to a feast, and who after the feast chewed heliotrope blossoms to make the breath of their lungs odoriferous. He felt also the beauty of Cicero's periods, and of verses of Horace or Ovid.

Educated by an Athenian rhetor, he conversed in Greek fluently; he knew whole pages of the "Iliad" by heart, and during a feast could sing odes of Anacreon till he had grown hoarse or drunk. Through his master and other rhetors he had rubbed against philosophy, and become sufficiently acquainted with it to know the plans of various edifices of thought reared in Hellas and the colonies; he understood too that all these edifices were in ruins. He knew many Stoics personally; for these he cherished dislike, since he looked on them rather as a political party, and, besides, as hypochondriacs, hostile to joyous living. Sceptics had a seat frequently at his table; and during intervals between courses they overturned entire systems, and announced at their cups, filled with wine, that pleasure was vanity, truth something unattainable, and that the object of a sage could be only dead rest.

All this struck Cinna's ears without piercing to the depth. He recognized no principle, and would have none. In Cato he saw the union of great character and great folly. He looked on life as a sea, on which winds blew whithersoever they listed; and wisdom in his eyes was the art of setting sails in such fashion that they would urge one's boat forward. He esteemed his own broad shoulders and sound stomach; he esteemed his own beautiful Roman head, with his aquiline nose and powerful jaws. He was certain that with these he could pass through life somehow.

Though not belonging to the school of Sceptics, he was a practical Sceptic and hence a lover of pleasure, though he knew that pleasure was not happiness. The genuine teaching of Epicurus he did not know; hence he considered himself an Epicurean. In general he looked on philosophy as mental fencing, as useful as that which was taught by the sword-master. When discourses on it wearied him, he went to the circus to see blood.

He did not believe in the gods any more than in virtue, truth, and happiness. He believed only in soothsaying, and had his own superstitions; moreover, the mysterious beliefs of the Orient roused his curiosity. To slaves he was a good master, unless when occasional tedium brought him to cruelty. He thought life a great amphora, which was the more valuable the better the wine contained in it; hence he tried to fill his own with the best. He did not love any one, but he loved many things, among others his own eagle-like face with splendid skull, and his shapely patrician foot.

In the first years of his frolicking life he loved also to astound Rome, and succeeded a number of times. Later he grew as indifferent to that as to other things.

CHAPTER II

At last he ruined himself. His creditors tore his property to pieces, and in place of it there remained to Cinna weariness, as after great toil, satiety, and one more unexpected thing, a certain deep disquiet. He had tried wealth; he had tried love, as that age understood it; he had tried pleasure, military glory, and dangers. He had come to know the limits of human thought more or less; he had come in contact with poetry and art. Hence he might suppose that from life he had taken what it had to give. Now he felt as though he had overlooked something—and that the most important. But he did not know what it was, and tortured his head over this problem in vain. More than once had he striven to shake himself out of these thoughts, and out of this disquiet. He had tried to persuade himself that there was nothing more in life, and could not be; but straightway his disquiet, instead of diminishing, increased quickly to such a degree that it seemed to him that he was disquieted not only for himself, but for all Rome. He envied the Sceptics and also considered them fools, for they insisted that one may fill completely the void with the empty. There existed in him then two men, as it were, one of whom was astonished at the disquiet which he felt, while the other was forced to recognize it as perfectly normal.

Soon after the loss of his property, thanks to great family influence, Cinna was sent to an official post in Alexandria, partly to build up a new fortune in a rich country. His disquiet entered the ship at Brundisium, and sailed across the sea with him. In Alexandria Cinna thought that questions concerning office, new people, another society, new impressions, would relieve him of the intrusive companion. But he was mistaken.

Two months passed, and just as the grain of Demeter, brought from Italy, grew still more luxuriantly in the rich soil of the Delta, so his disquiet from a sturdy twig changed, as it were, into a spreading cedar, and began to cast a still greater shadow on the soul of Cinna.

At first he strove to free himself of this shadow by the same life that he had led in Rome formerly. Alexandria was a place of pleasure, full of Grecian women with golden hair and clear complexions, which the Egyptian sun covered with a transparent, amber lustre. In their society he sought rest.

But when this also proved vain he began to think of suicide. Many of his comrades had freed themselves from life's cares in that manner, and for causes still more foolish than those which Cinna had,—frequently from weariness alone, from the emptiness of life, or a lack of desire to make further use of it. When a slave held a sword adroitly and with sufficient strength, one instant ended all. Cinna caught at this idea; but when he had almost resolved to obey it, a wonderful dream held him back. Behold, it seemed to him that when he was borne across the river he saw on the other bank his disquiet in the form of a wretched slave; it bowed to him, saying, "I have come in advance to receive thee." Cinna was terrified for the first time in life; because he understood that if he could not think of existence beyond the grave without disquiet, then they would both go there.

In this extreme, he resolved to make the acquaintance of sages with whom the Serapeum was crowded, judging that among them perhaps he might find the solution of his riddle. They, it is true, were unable to solve any doubt of his; but to make up they entitled him "of the museum," which title they offered usually to Romans of high birth and position. That was small consolation at first; and the stamp of sage, given a man who could not explain that which concerned him most highly, might seem to Cinna ironical. He supposed, however, that the Serapeum did not reveal all its wisdom at once, perhaps; and he did not lose hope altogether.

The most active sage in Alexandria was the noble Timon of Athens, a man of wealth, and a Roman citizen. He had lived a number of years in Alexandria, whither he had come to sound the depths of Egyptian science. It was said of him that there was no parchment or papyrus in the Library which he had not read, and that he possessed all the wisdom of mankind. He was, moreover, mild and forbearing. Cinna distinguished him at once among the multitude of pedants and commentators with stiffened brains, and soon formed with him an acquaintance which, after a time, was changed into close intimacy, and even into friendship. The young Roman admired the dialectic skill, the eloquence and dignity, with which the old man spoke of lofty themes touching man's destiny, and that of the world. He was struck especially by this, that that dignity was joined to a certain sadness. Later, when they had grown more intimate, Cinna was seized frequently by the wish to inquire of the old sage the cause of that sadness, and to open his own heart to him. In fact, it came to that finally.

CHAPTER III

A certain evening, after animated discussions about the transmigration of souls, they remained alone on the terrace, from which the view was toward the sea. Cinna, taking Timon's hand, declared openly what the great torment of his life was, and why he had striven to approach the scholars and philosophers of the Serapeum.

"I have gained this much at least," said he; "I have learned to know you, O Timon, and I understand now that if you cannot solve my life's riddle, no other man can."

Timon gazed for a time at the smooth surface of the sea, in which the new moon was reflected; then he said,—

"Hast thou seen those flocks of birds, Cinna, which fly past here in winter from northern glooms? Dost thou know what they seek in Egypt?"

"I do. Warmth and light."

"Souls of men also seek warmth, which is love, and light, which means truth. The birds know whither they are flying for their good; but souls are flying over roadless places, in wandering, in sadness, and disquiet."

"Why can they not find the road, noble Timon?"

"Once man's repose was in the gods; to-day, faith in the gods is burnt out, like oil in a lamp. Men thought that to souls philosophy would be the light of truth; to-day, as thou knowest best of all, on its ruins in Rome and in the Academy in Athens, and here, sit Sceptics, to whom it seemed that it was bringing in peace, but it brought in disquiet. For to renounce light and heat is to leave the soul in darkness, which is disquiet. Hence, stretching out our hands before us, we seek an exit in groping."

"Hast thou not found it?"

"I have sought, and I have not found it. Thou hast sought it in pleasure, I in thought; and the same mist encircles us. Know then that not thou alone art suffering, but in thee the soul of the world is tortured. Is it long since thou hast ceased to believe in the gods?"

"At Rome they are honored publicly yet, and even new ones are brought from Asia and Egypt; but no one believes in them sincerely, except dealers in vegetables, who come in the morning from the country to the city."

"And these are the only people who live in peace."

"They are like those who bow down here to cats and onions."

"Just like those, who, in the manner of beasts, ask for nothing beyond sleep after eating."

"But is life worth the living in view of this?"

"Do I know what death will bring?"

"What is the difference, then, between thee and the Sceptics?"

"Sceptics are satisfied with darkness, or feign that they are satisfied, but I suffer in it."

"And thou seest no salvation?"

Timon was silent for a moment, and then answered slowly, as if with hesitation,—

"I wait for it."

"Whence?"

"I know not."

Then he rested his head on the palm of his hand; and as if under the influence of that silence which had settled down on the terrace, he began to speak in a low and measured voice,—

"A wonderful thing; but at times it seems to me that if the world contained nothing beyond that which we know, and if we could be nothing more than we are, this disquiet would not exist in us. So in this sickness I find hope of health. Faith in Olympus and philosophy are dead, but health may be some new truth which I know not."

Beyond expectation, that talk brought great solace to Cinna. When he heard that the whole world was sick, and not he alone, he felt as if some one had taken a great weight from him and distributed it on a thousand shoulders.

CHAPTER IV

From that time the friendship uniting Cinna and the old Greek became still more intimate. They visited each other frequently and exchanged thoughts, like bread in time of a banquet. Besides, Cinna, in spite of experience and the weariness which comes of use, had not reached the age yet when life has ceased to contain the charm of unknown things; and just this charm he found in Antea, Timon's only daughter.

Her fame was not less in Alexandria than the fame of her father. Eminent Romans frequenting Timon's house did her homage, Greeks did her homage, philosophers from the Serapeum did her homage, and so did the people. Timon did not restrict her to the gineceum, after the manner of other women; and he tried to transfer to her everything that he himself knew. When she had passed the years of childhood, he read Greek books with her, and even Latin and Hebrew; for, gifted with an uncommon memory, and reared in many-tongued Alexandria, she learned those languages quickly. She was a companion to him in thoughts; she took frequent part in the discussions which were held in Timon's house during Symposiums. Often in the labyrinth of difficult questions, she was able, like Ariadne, to avoid going astray herself and to extricate others. Her father honored and admired her. The charm of mystery and almost of sacredness surrounded her, besides; for she had prophetic dreams, in which she saw things invisible to common mortals. The old sage loved her as his own soul, and the more for this reason, that he was afraid of losing her; for frequently she said that beings appeared in dreams to her,—ominous beings,—also a certain divine light, and she knew not whether this light was the source of life or death.

Meanwhile she was met only by love. The Egyptians, who frequented Timon's house, called her the Lotus; perhaps because that flower received divine honor on the banks of the Nile, and perhaps also because whoever saw it might forget the whole world besides.

Her beauty was equal to her wisdom. The Egyptian sun did not darken her face, in which the rosy rays of light seemed to be enclosed in transparent mother-of-pearl. Her eyes had the blueness of the Nile, and their glances flowed from a remoteness as unknown as the source of that mysterious river. When Cinna saw and heard her the first time, on returning home, he conceived the wish to rear an altar to her in the atrium of his house, and offer a white dove on it. He had met thousands of women in his life, beginning with virgins from the remote north, with white eye-lashes and hair the color of ripe wheat, and ending with Numidians, black as lava; but he had not met hitherto such a figure, or such a soul. And the oftener he saw her, the better he knew her, the oftener it happened to him to hear her words, the more did amazement increase in him. Sometimes he, who did not believe in the gods, thought that Antea could not be the daughter of Timon, but of a god, hence only half woman, and therefore half immortal.

And soon he loved her with a love unexpected, immense, irresistible, as different from the feeling which he had known up to that time as Antea was different from other women. He desired to love her only to do her honor. Hence he was willing to give blood to possess her. He felt that he would prefer to be a beggar with her than to be Caesar without her. And as a whirlpool of the sea sweeps away with irresistible might all that comes within its circle, so Cinna's love swept away his soul, his heart, his thoughts, his days, his nights, and everything out of which life is composed.

Till at last it swept away Antea.

"*Tu felix* (Thou art happy), Cinna!" said his friends.

"*Tu felix*, Cinna," said he to himself; and when at last he married her, when her divine lips uttered the sacramental words, "Where thou art, Caius, there am I, Caia," it seemed to him that his felicity was like the sea,—inexhaustible and boundless.

CHAPTER V

A year passed, and that young wife received at her domestic hearth almost divine honor; to her husband she was the sight of his eyes, love, wisdom, light. But Cinna, comparing his happiness with the sea, forgot that the sea has its ebbs.

After a year Antea fell into an illness cruel and unknown. Her dreams changed into terrible visions, which exhausted her life. In her face the rays of light were quenched; there remained only the paleness of mother-of-pearl. Her hands began to be transparent; her eyes sank deeply under her forehead; and the rosy lotus became more and more a white lotus, white as the face of the dead. It was noticed that falcons began to circle above Cinna's house, which in Egypt was a herald of death. The visions grew more and more terrible.

When at midday the sun filled the world with bright light, and the city was buried in silence, it seemed to Antea that she heard around her the quick steps of invisible beings, and in the depth of the air she saw a dry, yellow, corpse-like face gazing with black eyes at her. Those eyes gazed persistently, as if summoning her to go somewhere into a darkness full of mysteries and dread. Then Antea's body began to tremble, as in a fever; her forehead was covered with pallor, with drops of cold sweat; and that honored priestess of the domestic hearth was changed into a helpless and terrified child, who, hiding on her husband's breast, repeated with pale lips,—

"Save me, O Caius! defend me!"

And Caius would have hurled himself at every spectre which Persephone might send from the nether world, but in vain did he strain his eyes into space round about. As is usual in midday hours, it was lonely. White light filled the city; the sea seemed to burn in the sun, and in the silence was heard only the calling of falcons circling above the house.

The visions grew more and more frequent, and at last they came daily. They pursued Antea in the interior of the house, as well as in the atrium and the chambers. Cinna, by advice of physicians, brought in Egyptian sambuka players, and Bedouins, blowing clay whistles; the noisy music of these was to drown the sound made by the invisible beings. But all this proved futile. Antea heard the sound amid the greatest uproar; and when the sun became so high that a man's shadow was near his feet, like a garment hanging from the arm, in the air quivering from heat appeared the face of the corpse, and looking at Antea with glassy eyes it moved away gradually, as if to say, "Follow me!"

Sometimes it seemed to Antea that the lips of the corpse moved slowly; sometimes that black disgusting beetles came out from between them and flew through the air toward her. At the very thought of that vision her eyes were filled with terror, and at last life became such a dreadful torture that she begged Cinna to hold a sword for her, or to let her drink poison.

But he knew that he had not strength for the deed. With that very sword he would have opened his own veins to serve Antea, but he could not take her life. When he imagined that dear face of hers dead, with closed eyes, filled with icy composure, and that breast opened with his sword, he felt that he must go mad before he could kill her.

A certain Greek physician told him that Hecate appeared to Antea, and that those invisible beings whose noise frightened the sick woman were the attendants of the ominous divinity.

According to him, there was no salvation for Antea, for whoso has seen Hecate must die.

Then Cinna, who not long before would have laughed at faith in Hecate, sacrificed a hecatomb to her. But the sacrifice was useless, and next day the gloomy eyes were gazing at Antea about midday.

Attendants covered her head; but she saw the face even through the thickest covering. Then they confined her in a dark room; the face looked at her from the walls, illuminating the darkness with its pale gleam of a corpse.

Every evening the sick woman grew better, and fell into such a deep sleep that to Cinna and Timon it seemed more than once as though she would not wake again. Soon she grew so weak that she could not walk without assistance. She was borne about in a litter.

Cinna's former disquiet returned with a hundredfold greater force and took complete possession of him. He was terrified regarding the life of Antea; but there was also a wonderful feeling that her sickness was in some way mysteriously connected with that of which he had spoken in his first conversation with Timon. Perhaps the old sage had the same thought; but Cinna would not ask him, and feared to talk concerning this matter.

Meanwhile the sick woman withered like a flower in whose cup a poisonous spider has settled.

But the despairing Cinna strove against hope to save her. First he took her to the desert near Memphis; but when a stay in the quiet of the pyramids gave no respite from the dreadful visions, he returned to Alexandria and surrounded her with soothsayers, who professed to enchant away diseases. He brought in from every kind of shameless rabble people who exploited the credulity of mankind by marvellous medicines. But he had no choice left, and snatched at every method.

At this time there came from Caesarea a renowned physician, a Hebrew, Joseph, son of Khuza. Cinna brought him at once to his wife, and for a time hope returned to his heart. Joseph, who had no faith in Greek and Roman gods, rejected contemptuously the opinion about Hecate. He supposed it more likely that demons had entered the sick woman, and advised Cinna to leave Egypt, where, in addition to demons, marshy effluvia of the Delta might injure Antea. He advised also, perhaps because he was a Hebrew, to go to Jerusalem,—a place where demons have no entrance, and where the air is dry and wholesome.

Cinna followed this advice the more willingly,—first, because there was no other, and second, because Jerusalem was governed by an acquaintance of his, a procurator whose ancestors were formerly clients of the house of Cinna.

In fact, when they came, the procurator, Pontius, received them with open arms and gave them as dwelling his own summer residence, which stood near the walls of the city. But Cinna's hope was swept away before his arrival. The corpse-like face looked at Antea even on the deck of the galley; on coming to the city the sick woman waited for midday with the same deathly terror as on a time in Alexandria.

And so their days began to pass in oppression, despair, and fear of death.

CHAPTER VI

In the atrium, in spite of the fountain, the shady portico, and the early hour, it was extremely hot, for the marble was heated by the spring sun; but at a distance from the house there grew an old, branching pistachio-tree, which shaded a considerable area round about. As the place was open, the breeze there was far greater than elsewhere; hence Cinna commanded to carry to that spot the litter, decked with hyacinths and apple-blossoms, in which Antea was resting. Then sitting near her, he placed his palm on her hands, which were as pale as alabaster, and asked,—

"Is it pleasant for thee here, carissima?"

"Pleasant," answered she, in a scarcely audible voice.

And she closed her eyes, as if sleep had seized her. Silence followed. Only the breeze moved with a rustling the branches of the pistachio-tree; and on the earth around the litter were quivering golden spots, formed of sun-rays, which broke through between the leaves; locusts were hissing among the rocks.

The sick woman opened her eyes after a moment.

"Caius," said she, "is it true that in this country a philosopher has appeared, who cures the sick?"

"They call such men prophets here," answered Cinna. "I have heard of him, and I wished to bring him to thee, but it turned out that he was a false miracle-worker. Besides, he blasphemed against the sanctuary and the religion of this country; hence the procurator has delivered him to death, and this very day he is to be crucified."

Antea dropped her head.

"Time will cure thee," said Cinna, seeing the sadness reflected on her face.

"Time is at the service of death, not of life," answered she, slowly.

And again silence ensued; round about the golden spots quivered continually; the locusts hissed still more loudly, and from the crannies of the cliff little lizards crept out onto stones, and sought sunny places.

Cinna looked from moment to moment at Antea, and for the thousandth time despairing thoughts flew through his head. He felt that all means of salvation had been spent, that there was no ray of hope, that soon the dear form before him would become a vanishing shadow and a handful of dust in a columbarium.

Even now while lying with closed eyes in the litter decked with flowers, she seemed dead.

"I will follow thee!" said Cinna, in his soul.

Meanwhile steps were heard in the distance. Immediately Antea's face became white as chalk; from between her half-open lips came hurried breathing; her bosom heaved quickly. The ill-fated martyr felt sure that the crowd of invisible beings which preceded the corpse with glassy eyes were drawing near. Cinna seized her hands and strove to pacify her.

"Fear not, Antea; I hear those steps too. That is Pontius, who is coming to visit us," added he, after a while. In fact, the procurator, attended by two slaves, appeared at the turn of the path. He was a man no longer young; he had an oval face carefully shaven, full of assumed dignity, and also of suffering and care.

"A greeting to thee, noble Cinna, and to thee, divine Antea!" said he, as he came under the shade of the pistachio-tree. "After a cold night the day has grown hot. May it favor you both, and may the health of Antea bloom like those hyacinths and those apple-tree twigs, which adorn her litter."

"Peace be with thee, and be greeted!" answered Cinna.

The procurator seated himself on a piece of rock, looked at Antea, frowned imperceptibly, and answered,—

"Loneliness produces sadness and sickness; but in the midst of crowds there is no place for fear, hence I will give one advice to thee. Unfortunately this is neither Antioch nor Caesarea; there are no games here, no horse-races; and were we to erect a circus, those madmen would tear it down the next day. Here thou wilt hear nothing but this phrase, 'the law,' and everything disturbs that law. I would rather be in Scythia."

"Of what dost thou wish to speak, O Pilate?"

"Indeed, I have wandered from my subject; but cares are the cause of this. I have said that among crowds there is no room for fear. Now ye can have a spectacle to-day. In Jerusalem, ye should be amused with something; above all, Antea should be in the midst of crowds at midday. Three men will die on the cross to-day; that is better than nothing! Because of the Pasch a mob of the strangest ruffians has come from out all this land to the city. Ye can look at those people. I will command to give you a place apart near the crosses. I hope that the condemned will die bravely. One of them is a marvellous person: he calls himself the Son of God; he is as mild as a dove, and has really done nothing to merit death."

"And didst thou condemn him to the cross?"

"I wanted to rid myself of trouble, and also avoid stirring up that nest of hornets that buzz around the temple; even as it is, they send complaints to Rome against me. Besides, the accused is not a Roman citizen."

"The man will not suffer less for that reason."

The procurator made no answer, but after a while he began to speak, as if to himself,—

"There is one thing that I do not like,—exaggeration. Whoever uses that word before me takes away my cheerfulness for the day. The golden mean! that is what wisdom commands us to follow, as I think. And there is not a corner of the world in which that principle is less respected than here. How all this tortures me! how it tortures me! In nothing is there repose, in nothing balance,—neither in men nor in nature. At present, for example, it is spring; the nights are cold; but during the day there is such heat that it is difficult to walk on stones. It is long yet till midday, and see what is happening! Of the people—better not speak! I am here, because I must be here. Never mind that! I might leave my subject a second time. Go to witness the crucifixion. I am convinced that that Nazarene will die valiantly. I gave command to flog him, thinking in that way to save him from death. I am not cruel. When he was lashed he was as patient as a lamb, and he blessed the people. When he was covered with blood, he raised his eyes and prayed. That is the most marvellous person that I have seen in my life. My wife has not given me a moment of peace because of him. 'Permit not the death of that innocent man!' this is what she has been dinning into my ears since daybreak. I wanted to save him. Twice I went to the bema and spoke to those priests and that mangy rabble. They answered in one voice, raising their heads and opening their jaws to the ears, 'Crucify him!'"

"Didst thou yield to them?" asked Cinna.

"I did, for in the city there would be mobs, and I am here to keep peace. I must do my duty. I dislike exaggeration, and, besides, I am mortally wearied; but when I undertake a thing, I do not hesitate to sacrifice the life of one man for the general welfare, especially when he is an unknown person whom no one will mention. All the worse for him that he is not a Roman."

"The sun shines not on Rome alone," whispered Antea.

"Divine Antea," answered the procurator, "I might answer that on the whole round of the earth the sun shines on Roman rule; therefore for the good of that rule it is proper to sacrifice everything, and disturbances undermine our authority. But, above all, I beg of thee not to ask me to change the sentence. Cinna will tell thee that that cannot be, and that, once sentence is pronounced, Caesar alone can change it. Though I wished, I have not the power to change. Is that not the case, Caius?"

"It is."

But those words caused Antea evident pain, for she said, thinking of herself, perhaps,—

"Then it is possible to suffer and die without being guilty."

"No one is without guilt," answered Pontius. "This Nazarene has committed no crime; hence I, as procurator, washed my hands. But as a man, I condemn his teaching. I conversed with him purposely rather long, wishing to test the man, and convinced myself that he announces monstrous things. The case is difficult! The world must stand on sound sense. Who denies that virtue is needed? Certainly not I. But even the Stoics only teach men to endure opposition with calmness; they do not insist that we should renounce everything, from our property to our dinner. Answer, Cinna,—thou art a man of sound judgment,—what wouldst thou think of me were I, neither from one cause nor another, to bestow this house in which thou art dwelling on those tattered fellows who warm themselves in the sun at the Joppa gate? And he insists on just such things. Besides, he says that we should love all equally: the Jews as well as the Romans themselves, the Romans as the Egyptians, the Egyptians as the Africans, and so on. I confess that I have had enough of this. At the moment when his life is in peril, he bears himself as if the question were of some one else; he teaches—and prays. It is not my duty to save a man who has no care for his own safety. Whoso does not know how to preserve measure in anything is not a man of judgment. Moreover, he calls himself the Son of God, and disturbs the foundations on which society rests, and therefore harms people. Let him think what he likes in his soul, if he will not raise disturbance. As a man, I protest against his teaching. If I do not believe in the gods, let us concede that it is my affair. Still I recognize the use of religion, and I declare so publicly, for I judge that religion is a curb on people. Horses must be harnessed, and harnessed securely. Finally, death should not be terrible to that Nazarene, for he declares that he will rise from the dead."

Cinna and Antea looked at each other with amazement.

"That he will rise from the dead?"

"Neither more nor less; after three days. So at least his disciples declare. I forgot to ask him myself. For that matter, it is all one, since death liberates a man from promises. And even should he not rise from the dead, he will lose nothing, since, according to his teaching, genuine happiness and eternal life begin only after death. He speaks of this, indeed, as a man perfectly certain. In his Hades it is brighter than in the world under the sun, and whoso suffers more in this world will enter that with greater certainty; he must only love, and love, and love."

"A wonderful doctrine," said Antea.

"And these people here cry to thee, 'Crucify him!'?" inquired Cinna.

"And I do not even wonder at this, for hatred is the soul of this people, for what, if not hatred, can demand that love be crucified?"

Antea rubbed her forehead with her emaciated hand.

"And is he certain that it is possible to live and be happy after death?"

"That is why neither the cross nor death terrify him."

"How good that would be, Caius!"

"How does he know this?" inquired she, after a while.

The procurator waved his hand: "He says that he knows it from the Father of all, who for the Jews is the same as Jove for us, with this difference, that, according to the Nazarene, the Father alone is one and merciful."

"How good that would be, Caius!" repeated the sick woman.

Cinna opened his lips as if to make some answer, but remained silent; and the conversation stopped. Evidently Pontius was continuing to think of the strange doctrine of the Nazarene, for he shook his head and shrugged his shoulders repeatedly. At last he rose and began to take leave.

All at once Antea said,—

"Caius, let us go to look at that Nazarene."

"Hasten," said Pilate, as he was going away; "the procession will move soon."

CHAPTER VII

The day, hot and bright from early morning, was obscured about midday. From the northeast clouds were rolling up, either dark or copper-colored, not over large, but dense, as if pregnant with a tempest. Between them the deep blue of the sky was still visible, but it was easy to foresee that they would soon pack together and conceal the whole round of the sky. Meanwhile the sun covered the edges of them with fire and gold. Over the city itself and the adjacent hills there extended yet a broad space of clear blue, and in the valley there was no breath of wind.

On the lofty platform of ground called Golgotha stood here and there small groups of people who had preceded the procession which was to move from the city. The sun illuminated broad, stony spaces, which were empty, gloomy, and barren; their monotonous pearl-color was interrupted only by the black net of ravines and gullies, the blacker because the platform itself was covered with light. In the distance were visible more elevated eminences, equally empty, veiled by the blue haze of distance.

Lower down, between the walls of the city and the platform of Golgotha, lay a plain bordered in places with cliffs less naked. From crannies in which had collected some little fertile earth, fig-trees peeped forth with few and scant leaves. Here and there rose flat-roofed buildings fixed to the cliff-side, like swallows' nests to stone walls, or shining from afar in the sun-rays were sepulchres, painted white. At present, because of the approaching holidays and the concourse of provincials in the capital, multitudes of huts and tents had been raised near the city walls; these formed whole encampments filled with men and camels.

The sun rose ever higher on that expanse of heaven which was still free from clouds. The hours were approaching in which usually deep silence reigned on those heights, for every living creature sought refuge inside the walls or within the ravines. And even at this time, in spite of uncommon animation, there was a certain sadness in that neighborhood in which the dazzling light fell not on green, but on gray stone expanses. The noise of distant voices, coming from the direction of the walls, was changed into the sound of waves, as it were, and seemed to be swallowed by the silence.

The single groups of people waiting on Golgotha since morning turned their faces toward the city, whence the procession might move at any moment. Antea's litter arrived; a few soldiers, sent by the procurator, preceded it. These were to open a way through the multitude, and in case of need restrain from deeds of disrespect the fanatical throng, and those who hated foreigners. At the side of the litter walked Cinna, in company with the centurion Rufilus.

Antea was calmer, less frightened than usual at the approach of midday, and with it the terror of dreadful visions, which had drawn the life out of her. What the procurator had said touching the young Nazarene, had attracted her mind and turned attention from her own misery. For her there was in this something wonderful which she could hardly understand. The world of that time had seen many persons die as calmly as a funeral pile quenches when the fuel in it is consumed. But that was a calmness coming from bravery, or from a philosophic agreement with the implacable necessity of exchanging light for darkness, real life for an existence misty, vanishing, and indefinite. No one up to that time had blessed death; no one had died with unshaken certainty that only after the funeral pyre or the grave would real life begin,—life as mighty and endless as only a being all-powerful and eternal can give.

And he whom they had appointed for crucifixion declared this as an undoubted truth. This teaching not only struck Antea, but seemed to her the only source of consolation. She knew that she must die, and immense regret seized her. For what did death mean for her? It meant to lose Cinna, to lose her father, to lose the world, to lose love, for a cold, empty gloom, which was half nothing. Hence the more desirable it was for her in life, the greater must be her sorrow. If death could be good for anything, or if it were possible to take with her even the remembrance of love, or the memory of happiness, she would be able to gain resignation the more quickly.

Then, while she expected nothing from death, she heard all at once that it could give everything. And who had made that announcement? A certain wonderful man, a teacher, a prophet, a philosopher, who enjoined love as the highest virtue, who blessed people when they were lashing him; and this man they had condemned to the cross. Hence Antea thought: "Why did he teach thus if the cross was his only reward? Others desired power; he did not desire it. Others desired wealth; he remained poor. Others desired palaces, feasts, excesses, purple robes, and chariots inlaid with mother-of-pearl and ivory; he lived like a shepherd. Meanwhile he enjoined love, compassion, poverty; therefore he could not be malicious and deceive people purposely. If he spoke the truth, let death be blessed as the end of earthly misery, as the change from a lower to a loftier happiness, as light for eyes that are quenching, as wings with which one flies away into endless bliss!"

Antea understood then what the promise of resurrection signified. The mind and heart of the poor sick woman cleaved with all their strength to that teaching. She recalled also the words of her father, who had repeated more than once that some new truth might bring the tortured soul of man out of darkness and imprisonment. And here was the new truth! It had conquered death; hence it had brought salvation. Antea sank with her whole being in those thoughts; so that for many and many a day Cinna for the first time failed to find terror in her face at the approach of midday.

The procession moved at last from the city toward Golgotha. From the height where Antea was sitting, it could be seen perfectly. The crowd, though considerable, seemed lost on those stony expanses. Through the open gate of Jerusalem flowed more and more people, and on the way they were joined by those who had been waiting outside the walls. They went at first in a long line, which, as it moved forward, spread like a swollen river. At both sides were running swarms of children.

The procession was made varied and many-colored by the white tunics and the scarlet and blue kerchiefs of women. In the centre were glittering the arms and spears of Roman soldiers, on which the sun cast fleeting rays, as it were. The uproar of mingled voices came from afar and rose with increasing distinctness.

At last the multitude came quite near; the first ranks began to ascend the height. The throng of people hurried on so as to occupy the nearest places and see the torment more clearly; because of this the division of soldiers, conducting the condemned, fell more and more toward the rear. Children arrived first, mainly boys, half naked, with cloths fastened around their hips, with shaven heads, except two tufts of hair near the temple, embrowned, with eyes almost blue, and harsh voices. In the wild uproar they fell to pulling out of the crannies bits of stone broken from the cliffs; these they wished to throw at those who were to be crucified. Right after them the height swarmed with a nondescript rabble. Their faces were for the greater part excited by the movement and by the hope of a spectacle. On no face was there a sign of compassion. The noise of rasping voices, the endless number of words thrown out by each mouth, the suddenness of their movements, astonished Antea, though accustomed in Alexandria to the word-loving liveliness of Greeks. Before her, people spoke as if they wished to hurl themselves at one another. They screamed as if escaping death; they resisted as if some one were flaying them.

The centurion Rufilus, approaching the litter, gave explanations in a calm, official voice. Meanwhile new waves flowed up from the city. The throng increased every moment. In the crowd were seen wealthy men of Jerusalem, dressed in girded tunics, holding themselves aloof from the wretched rabble of the suburbs. In numbers also came villagers which the festival had brought to the city, with their families; field-workers, with kindly and astonished faces, came, bearing bags at their girdles; shepherds came, dressed in goat-skins. Crowds of women came with the men; but as wives of the more wealthy citizens did not leave their homes willingly, these women were chiefly of the people. They were villagers, or women of the street; these last dressed gaudily, had dyed hair, brows, and nails; they wore immense ear-rings and coin necklaces, and gave out from a distance the odor of nard.

The Sanhedrim arrived at last; and in the midst of it, Annas, an aged man with the face of a vulture and eyes with red lids; then appeared the unwieldy Caiaphas, wearing a two-horned hat, with a gilded tablet on his breast. With these walked various Pharisees; as, for instance, those who "drag their legs" and strike every obstacle purposely with their feet; Pharisees with "bloody foreheads," who beat those foreheads against the wall, also by design; and Pharisees "bent over," as if to receive the burden of the sins of the whole city on their shoulders. Gloomy importance and cold vindictiveness distinguished them from the noisy rabble.

Cinna looked at this throng of people with the cool, contemptuous visage of a man of the ruling race, Antea with astonishment and fear. Many Jews inhabited Alexandria, but there they were half Hellenized; here for the first time she saw Jews as the procurator had described them, and as they were in their own native nest. Her youthful face, on which death had imprinted its stamp, her form, resembling a shadow, attracted general attention. They stared at her with insolence in so far as the soldiers surrounding her litter permitted them; and so great among them was contempt for foreigners that no compassion was evident in the eyes of any; rather did gladness shine in them because the victim would not escape death. Then the daughter of Timon understood for the first time, and precisely, why those people demanded a cross for the prophet who had proclaimed love.

And all at once that Nazarene appeared to Antea as some one so near that he was almost dear to her. He had to die, and so had she. Nothing could save him now, after the issuing of the sentence, and sentence had fallen also on her; hence it seemed to Antea that the brotherhood of misfortune and death had united them. But he approached the cross with faith in a morrow after death. She had not that faith yet, and had come to obtain it from the sight of him.

Meanwhile from afar was heard an uproar, a whistling, a howling, then all was silent. Next came clatter of weapons and the heavy tread of legionaries. The crowds swayed, opened, and the division conducting the condemned began to push past the litter. In front, at both sides, and behind, advanced soldiers with slow and measured tread. Next were three arms of crosses, which seemed to move of themselves; they were borne by persons bent under the weight of them. It was easy to divine that the Nazarene was not among those three, for two had the insolent faces of thieves. The third was a simple countryman, no longer young; clearly the soldiers had impressed him to do work for another.

The Nazarene walked behind the crosses; two soldiers marched near him. He wore a purple mantle thrown over his garments, and a crown of thorns, from under the points of which drops of blood issued; of these some flowed slowly along his face, others had grown stiff under the crown, in the form of berries of the wild rose, or coral beads. He was pale, and moved forward with slow, unsteady, and weakened step. He advanced amid insults from the multitude, sunk, as it were, in the meditation of another world; he was as if seized away from the earth altogether, as if not caring for the cries of hatred, or as if forgiving beyond the measure of human forgiveness and compassionate beyond the measure of human compassion, for, embraced now by infinity, raised above human estimate, he was exceedingly mild, and was sorrowful only through his measureless sorrow for all men.

"Thou art Truth," whispered Antea, with trembling lips.

The retinue was passing just near the litter. It halted for a moment while soldiers in front were clearing the road of the throng; Antea saw then the Nazarene a few steps away. She saw the breeze move his hair; she saw the ruddy reflection from his mantle on his pallid and almost transparent face. The mob, rushing toward him, surrounded with a dense half-circle the soldiers, who had to resist with spears, to save him from their rage. Everywhere were visible outstretched arms with clinched fists, eyes bursting through their lids, gleaming teeth, beards thrown apart from mad movements, and foaming lips through which came hoarse shouts.

But he looked around, as if wishing to ask, "What have I done to you?" then he raised his eyes to heaven and prayed—and forgave.

"Antea! Antea!" cried Cinna at that moment.

But Antea seemed not to hear his cries. Great tears were falling from her eyes; she forgot her sickness, forgot that for many days she had not risen from the litter; and sitting up on a sudden, trembling, half conscious, from pity, compassion, and indignation at the mad shrieks of the multitude, she took hyacinths with apple blossoms and cast them before the feet of the Nazarene.

For a moment there was silence. Amazement seized the crowd at sight of this noble Roman lady giving honor to the condemned. He turned his eyes to her poor sick face, and his lips began to move, as if blessing her. Antea fell again on the pillow of the litter; she felt that a sea of light, of goodness, of grace, of consolation, of hope, of happiness, was falling on her.

"Thou art Truth," whispered she, a second time.

Then a new wave of tears came to her eyes.

But they pushed him forward to a place a few tens of steps distant from the litter; on that place stood already the uprights of crosses, fixed in a cleft of the rocky platform. The crowd concealed him again; but, since that place was elevated considerably, Antea soon saw his pale face and the crown of thorns. The legionaries turned once more toward the rabble, which they clubbed away, lest it might interrupt the execution. They began then to fasten the two thieves to the side crosses. The third cross stood in the middle; to the top of it was fastened, with a nail, a white card which the growing wind pulled and raised. When soldiers, approaching the Nazarene at last, began to undress him, shouts rose in the crowds: "King! king! do not yield! King, where are thy legions? Defend thyself!" At moments laughter burst forth,—laughter that bore away the multitude till on a sudden the whole stony height resounded with one roar. Then they stretched him face upward on the ground, to nail his hands to the arms of the cross, and raise him afterward with it to the main pillar.

Thereupon some man, in a white tunic, standing not far from the litter, cast himself on the earth suddenly, gathered dust and bits of stone on his head, and cried in a shrill despairing voice, "I was a leper, and he cured me; why do ye crucify him?"

Antea's face became white as a kerchief.

"He cured that man; dost hear, Caius?" said she.

"Dost wish to return?" asked Cinna.

"No! I will remain here!"

But a wild and boundless despair seized Cinna because he had not called the Nazarene to his house to cure Antea.

At that moment the soldiers, placing nails at his hands, began to strike. The dull clink of iron against iron was heard; this soon changed into a sound which went farther, for the points of the nails, having passed through flesh, entered the wood. The crowds were silent again, perhaps to enjoy cries which torture might bring from the mouth of the Nazarene. But he remained silent, and on the height was heard only the ominous and dreadful sound of the hammers.

At last they had finished the work, and the cross-piece was drawn up, with the body. The centurion in charge pronounced, or rather sang out monotonously, words of command, in virtue of which a soldier began to nail the feet.

At this moment those clouds, which since morning had been extending on the horizon, hid the sun. The distant hills and cliffs, which had been gleaming in brightness, gleamed no longer. The light turned to darkness. An ominous bronze-colored gloom seized the region about, and, as the sun sank more deeply behind piles of clouds, the gloom became denser. Men might have thought that some being from above was sifting down to the earth lurid darkness. The air now grew sultry.

All at once even those remnants of lurid gleams became black. Clouds, dark as night, rolled and pushed forward, like a gigantic wave, toward the height and the city. A tempest was coming! The world was filled with fear.

"Let us return!" said Cinna again.

"Once more, once more, I wish to see him," answered Antea.

Darkness had concealed the hanging bodies. Cinna gave command to carry the litter nearer the place of torment. They carried it so near that barely a few steps were between them and the cross. On the dark tree they saw the body of the Crucified, who in that general eclipse seemed made of silver rays of the moon. His breast rose with quick breathing. His face and eyes were turned upward yet.

Then from the rolls of clouds was heard a deep rumbling. Thunder was roused; it rose and rolled with tremendous report from the east to the west, and then falling, as if into a bottomless abyss, was heard farther and farther down, now dying away, and now increasing; at last it roared till the earth shook in its foundations.

A gigantic blue lightning-flash rent the clouds, lighted the sky, the earth, the crosses, the arms of the soldiers, and the mob huddled together, like a flock of sheep, filled with distress and terror.

After the lightning came deeper darkness. Close to the litter was heard the sobbing of women, who also drew near the cross. There was something ominous in this sobbing amid silence. Those who were lost in the multitude began now to cry out. Here and there were heard terrified voices,—

"O Yah! oj lanu! [woe to us!] O Yah! Have they not crucified the Just One?"

"Who gave true testimony! O Yah!"

"Who raised the dead!"

And another voice called,—

"Woe to thee, Jerusalem!"

Still another,—

"The earth trembles!"

A new lightning-flash disclosed the depths of the sky, and in them gigantic figures of fire, as it were. The voices were silent, or rather were lost in the whistling of the whirlwind, which sprang up all at once with tremendous force; it swept off a multitude of mantles and kerchiefs, and hurled them away over the height.

Voices cried out anew,—

"The earth trembles!"

Some began to flee. Terror nailed others to the spot; and they stood fixed in amazement, without thought, with this dull impression only,—that something awful was happening.

But, on a sudden, the gloom began to be less dense. Wind rolled the clouds over, twisted and tore them like rotten rags; brightness increased gradually. At last the dark ceiling was rent, and through the opening rushed in all at once a torrent of sunlight; presently the heights became visible, and with them the crosses and the terrified faces of the people.

The head of the Nazarene had fallen low on his breast; it was as pale as wax; his eyes were closed, his lips blue.

"He is dead," whispered Antea.

"He is dead," repeated Cinna.

At this moment a centurion thrust his spear into the side of the dead. A wonderful thing: the return of light and the sight of that death seemed to appease that crowd. They pushed nearer and nearer, especially since the soldiers did not bar approach. Among the throng were heard voices,—

"Come down from the cross! Come down from the cross!"

Antea cast her eyes once more on that low-hanging head, then she said, as if to herself,—

"Will he rise from the dead?"

In view of death, which had put blue spots on his eyes and mouth, in view of those arms stretched beyond measure, and in view of that motionless body which had settled down with the weight of dead things, her voice trembled with despairing doubt.

Not less was the disappointment rending Cinna's soul. He also believed not that the Nazarene would rise from the dead; but he believed that had he lived, he alone, with his power, good or evil, might have given health to Antea. Meanwhile more numerous voices were calling,—

"Come down from the cross! Come down from the cross!"

"Come down!" repeated Cinna, with despair. "Cure her for me; take my life!"

The air became purer and purer. The mountains were still in mist, but above the height and the city the sky had cleared perfectly. "Turris Antonia" glittered in sunlight as bright itself as the sun. The air had become fresh, and was full of swallows. Cinna gave command to return.

It was an afternoon hour. Near the house Antea said,—

"Hecate has not come to-day."

Cinna also was thinking of that.

CHAPTER VIII

The vision did not appear the next day. The sick woman was unusually animated, for Timon had come from Caesarea. Alarmed for the life of his daughter and frightened by Cinna's letters, he had left Alexandria a few days earlier to look once again on his only child before her parting. At Cinna's heart hope began to knock again, as if to give notice to receive it. But he had not courage to open the door to that guest; he did not dare to harbor hope.

In the visions which had been killing Antea, there had been intervals, it is true, not of two days, but of one in Alexandria, and in the desert. The present relief Cinna attributed to Timon's arrival, and her impressions at the cross, which so filled the sick woman's soul that she could talk of nothing else, even with her father.

Timon listened with attention; he did not contradict; he meditated and merely inquired carefully about the doctrine of the Nazarene, of which Antea knew, for that matter, only what the procurator had told her.

In general she felt healthier and somewhat stronger; and when midday had passed and gone, real solace shone in her eyes. She repeated that that was a favorable day, and begged her husband to make note of it.

The day was really sad and gloomy. Rain had begun in the early morning, at first very heavy, then fine and cutting, from low clouds which extended monotonously. Only in the evening did the sky break through, and the great fiery globe of the sun look out of the mists, paint in purple and gold the gray rocks, the white marble porticoes of the villas, and descend with endless gleams toward the Mediterranean.

The next morning was wonderfully beautiful. The weather promised to be warm, but the morning was fresh, the sky without a spot, and the earth so sunk in a blue bath that all objects seemed blue. Antea had given directions to bear her out and place her under the favorite pistachio-tree, so that from the elevation on which the tree stood she might delight herself with the view of the blue and gladsome distance.

Cinna and Timon did not move a step from the litter, and watched the face of the sick woman carefully. There was in it a certain alarm of expectation, but it was not that mortal fear which used to seize her at the approach of midday. Her eyes cast a more lively light, and her cheeks bloomed with a slight flush. Cinna thought indeed at moments that Antea might recover; and at this thought he wanted to throw himself on the ground, to sob from delight, and bless the gods. Then again he feared that that was perhaps the last gleam of the dying lamp. Wishing to gain hope from some source, he glanced every little while at Timon; but similar thoughts must have been passing through his head, for he avoided Cinna's glances. None of the three mentioned by a word that midday was near. But Cinna, casting his eyes every moment at the shadows, saw with beating heart that they were growing shorter and shorter.

And he sat as if sunk in thought. Perhaps the least alarmed was Antea herself. Lying in the open litter, her head rested on a purple pillow; she breathed with delight that pure air which the breeze brought from the west, from the distant sea. But before midday the breeze had ceased to blow. The heat increased; warmed by the sun, the pepperwort of the cliffs and the thickets of nard began to give out a strong and intoxicating odor. Bright butterflies balanced themselves over bunches of anemones. From the crevices of the rocks little lizards, already accustomed to that litter and those people, sprang out, one after the other, confident as usual, and also cautious in every movement. The whole world was enjoying that serene peace, that warmth, that calm sweetness and azure drowsiness.

Timon and Cinna seemed also to dissolve in that sunny rest. The sick woman closed her eyes as if a light sleep had seized her; and nothing interrupted that silence except sighs, which from time to time raised her breast.

Meanwhile Cinna noticed that his shadow had lost its lengthened form and was lying there under his feet.

It was midday.

All at once Antea opened her eyes and called out in a kind of strange voice,—

"Caius, give me thy hand."

He sprang up, and all the blood was stiffened to ice in his heart. The hour of terrible visions had come.

Her eyes opened wider and wider.

"Dost thou see," said she, "how light collects there and binds the air; how it trembles, glitters, and approaches me?"

"Antea, look not in that direction!" cried Cinna.

But, oh, wonder! there was no fear on her face. Her lips were parted; her eyes were gazing, and opening wider and wider; a certain immeasurable delight began to brighten her face.

"The pillar of light approaches me," said she. "See! that is he; that is the Nazarene!—he is smiling. O Mild! O Merciful! The transfixed hands he stretches out like a mother to me. Caius, he brings me health, salvation, and calls me to himself."

Cinna grew very pale, and said,—

"Whithersoever he calls us, let us follow him."

A moment later, on the other side, on the stony path leading to the city, appeared Pontius Pilate. Before he had come near, it was evident from his face that he was bringing news, which, as a man of judgment, he considered a fresh, absurd invention of the ignorant and credulous rabble. In fact, while still at some distance, he began to call, wiping perspiration from his brow,—

"Imagine to thyself, they declare that he has risen from the dead!"

www.ingramcontent.com/pod-product-compliance
Lightning Source LLC
Chambersburg PA
CBHW051011050726
47592CB00007B/2807

9781774819487